What Do You Know about Manners?

A Funny Quiz for Kids

by Cynthia MacGregor

with Christine Zuchora-Walske
art by Stephen Carpenter

...k Press

...mon & Schuster
New York

Library of Congress Cataloging-in-Publication Data

MacGregor, Cynthia.
    What do you know about manners?: a funny quiz for kids /
      Cynthia MacGregor.
        p. cm.
    Includes index.
    Summary: Multiple choice quizzes about polite behavior at home,
      at school, and with friends.
    ISBN 0-88166-354-9 (Meadowbrook)—ISBN 0-689-83292-3
      (Simon & Schuster)
      1. Etiquette for children and teenagers—United States—
        Miscellanea—Juvenile literature.
    [1. Etiquette—Miscellanea.] I. Title.
    BJ1857.C5 M124 2000
    395.1'22—dc21   99-089731

Editor: Christine Zuchora-Walske
Proofreader: Megan McGinnis
Editorial Assistant: Kelly Williams
Backup Goofballs: Carolyn Walske, Marisue Gleason
Production Manager: Joe Gagne
Desktop Publishing: Danielle White
Art: Stephen Carpenter

© 2000 by Cynthia MacGregor

Published by Meadowbrook Press, 5451 Smetana Drive, Minnetonka,
MN 55343

www.meadowbrookpress.com

BOOK TRADE DISTRIBUTION by Simon & Schuster, a division of Simon
and Schuster, Inc., 1230 Avenue of the Americas, New York, NY 10020

04 03 02 01 00   10 9 8 7 6 5 4 3 2 1

Printed in the United States of America

Dedication

To my mother, Yvonne, who did her
best to teach me good manners.
She certainly deserves the credit
when my manners are good.
But she's not to be held responsible
when they aren't—just blame me.

(Blaming someone else for my
mistakes wouldn't be good manners!)

Acknowledgments

Huge thanks to Vic Bobb,
a good writer and a good friend.

I am also grateful to my editor,
Christine Zuchora-Walske, whose
editing truly improved this book.

Contents

Introduction

Before you roll your eyes and use this book as a doorstop—wait! Yes, this is a book about manners. But it's nothing like the lectures (blah, blah) you may be used to hearing. This book is guaranteed to make you smile. I bet you'll even giggle!

Instead of *telling* you a zillion things you should do to show good manners, this book *asks* you what you would do in all kinds of different situations. After all, that's what manners are for: helping you handle all the ordinary and not-so-ordinary things that happen in your life. Using good manners isn't just knowing which fork to use at a fancy dinner or remembering to call the Queen of England "Your Highness." It's more like speaking the same language your family and friends speak so you can talk with them. Or following the rules when you play soccer so the game doesn't turn into a wild stampede. Or covering your mouth when you sneeze because you'd hate it if someone sneezed all over you! Good manners simply help people understand each other and get along.

If you like taking quizzes (the fun kind in magazines, not the icky math-class pop-quiz kind), you'll love this book. It contains one hundred multiple-choice questions about things that can happen to anybody. Most of the answers are a bit . . . well, okay . . . *really* goofy, so you'll have no trouble spotting the right answers unless you've been raised by chimpanzees. As you take the quiz, enjoy imagining the crazy things that can happen when people use bad manners. Keep track of your answers as you go and figure out your MQ (Manners Quotient) when you reach the end of the book. Then show your family and friends (without bragging, of course—that would be bad manners) just how smart and civilized you are!

Have fun!

Cynthia

Everyday Manners

There are hundreds of little things you can do every day to show good manners, but if I tried to talk about all of them in one chapter, it would be as long as a whole book! Instead, I'll just mention ten very important points. These are situations that happen so often, you probably don't even notice them! And now, here they are . . .

The Top Ten Ways to Prove You're Not a Chimpanzee!

You should say "excuse me" . . .

A. whenever you burp, accidentally bump into someone, or really need to interrupt someone.

B. if you tickle your little sister too long and she winds up wetting her pants.

C. whenever you copy a friend's test answers.

D. after you play a practical joke like putting a whoopee cushion on your teacher's chair.

Answer: A. "Excuse me" is useful for getting some-one's attention when you really need help and for keeping people from clobbering you when you goof up accidentally. It won't do you much good if you're being a pain on purpose, though. Even if you say "excuse me" to your teacher after playing a practical joke, you'll probably still end up at the principal's office. And if you try to excuse yourself for copying a friend's schoolwork, you'll give him or her a perfect excuse to stop being your friend! As for tickling your little sister . . . I know it's tempting, but don't tor-ture her too much—she might grow up to be twice as big as you!

"Please" . . .

A. is a magic word—use it, and the Wish Fairy will give you anything you want.

B. is a dumb extra word that makes it take longer to ask for something.

C. is a polite word that makes people more willing to listen to you.

D. rhymes with "fleas" and should be said only to itchy dogs.

Answer: C. Say "please" to your pooch if you want to, but Spot will probably just keep scratching. "Please" works a lot better on people. It's short for "if you please," which tells people you're paying attention to their feelings. They'll be more willing to do what you ask if they think you're a nice person. (Even if you're really not!)

Say "thank you" . . .

A. if you get a gift you really like and not something dorky like that hairy, itchy, ugly pink sweater Aunt Irma gave you last year for your birthday.

B. all the time at your friend's house, so your friend's parents will invite you back often. (They have such a great trampoline!)

C. whenever one of your parents elbows you to remind you.

D. whenever someone compliments you, gives you something, or does something for you.

Answer: D. (Well . . . C, too, but if you do D, you won't need C.) Thank anyone who says something nice to you or does something nice for you like giving you a present (even if you think it's dorky), telling you you're smart, or pointing out that you have spinach stuck in your teeth. You don't have to say "thank you" when someone pinches your cheek and says how much you've grown. (Try not to gag, though!)

4

You should write a thank-you note . . .

A. to anyone who gives you a birthday or holiday gift—just to make sure you get a gift from that person next year.

B. only when you get a gift you like. If someone gives you a gift you hate, write a "How could you be so stupid?" note.

C. for every little thing you get. If someone gives you a cookie, a phone call, or even a wedgie, write a thank-you note.

D. whenever someone gives you a gift or does something supernice for you.

Answer: D. If you write a thank-you note for every little thing you get, you'll use up a forest worth of paper—and maybe get carted off to a mental hospital. Just use thank-you notes to let people know you appreciate the time, effort, and/or money they've spent to give or do something really nice. Even if you don't like a gift, try to think of something good to say about it. For example, you can say that the hairy, itchy, ugly pink sweater you got from Aunt Irma reminds you of cotton candy, your favorite treat!

Don't interrupt when people are talking . . .

A. ever.

B. unless you've already interrupted them accidentally . . . say, by burping . . . then say "excuse me" quietly and let the other person go on talking.

C. unless it's urgent. For example, if you're at someone else's house, and you need to ask where the bathroom is—or if the cat has just stepped into a pan of hot lasagna —say "Excuse me for interrupting, but . . ."

D. unless they've been talking longer than ten minutes. Always wear a watch, so you can stop people when they've been yakking too long!

Answer: B and C. Hey, you're not the Yakking Police. But if you really need to use the bathroom, you might wind up doing something a lot worse than interrupting if you don't get there in time. If you've just burped while someone is talking to you, that person's going to think you're a real pig unless you excuse yourself. And that cat stuck in the lasagna needs help immediately! Just be sure you have a good reason for interrupting.

Talking quietly . . .

A. is totally useless. If you know something worth saying, say it so everyone within a mile of you can hear it!

B. is lots of fun. Speak really softly so people can't understand you and have to ask "What?" at least six times.

C. is much nicer indoors than talking **REALLY LOUDLY!**

D. is a great prank if you're also hiding. People will think they're hearing a ghost.

Answer: C. Most people can only stand to ask "What?" a couple of times before they get peeved and walk away, leaving you standing there alone, looking . . . well, pretty dumb. Saying everything as loudly as you can is likely to chase people away, too —or make them mad enough to shout back at you. Since it's usually pretty quiet indoors (unless your house is next-door to an airplane runway), people will hear you just fine—and like you a lot better—if you're sort of quiet, too.

Cussing or swearing . . .

A. shouldn't be done in church, because people who go to church don't know what cuss words mean and can't enjoy them.

B. is the perfect way to let off steam when you stub your toe.

C. bothers a lot of people.

D. is a great way to impress people with your big vocabulary.

Answer: C. Trust me: even if it's hard to imagine your parents, your pastor, and that prim old lady in the third pew swearing like sailors, everyone knows what cuss words mean. (Tip: Adults are much smarter than they look!) And most people—kids and adults —are bothered by cussing. So if you really need to let off some steam with a few choice words, do it where no one else can hear you. Or better yet, cuss creatively! Next time you stub your toe, instead of using those worn-out old cuss words, shout "Holy toe jam, Batman!" or "Fuzzbuckets!" or "Potassium permanganate!" The longer the words you use are, the less your toe will hurt by the time you're done saying them.

When others look especially nice or do something really well, you should . . .

A. tell them to stop showing off, then pinch them good and hard to get rid of those stuck-up smiles.

B. compliment them.

C. ignore them. They'll wonder what you want from them if you're too nice.

D. make yourself look better than they do by tripping them when they walk by.

Answer: B. Imagine what the world would be like if people never tried to look nice or do things well. We'd all be wandering around in our pajamas with bedhead and bad breath, riding buses that break down every ten seconds to buildings that crumble whenever you slam a door. When people make an effort to look nice or do things well, they make the world a much nicer place. Why not thank them by making them feel good? Give a compliment and pass a smile along— it'll make you feel good, too!

It's okay to brag . . .

A. when you've gotten a good report card.

B. when you know a secret (for example, that your friend mumbles "oogie-boogie" in her sleep).

C. when you get a new bike and you don't have to ride that hand-me-down with the Smurf decals and handlebar tassels anymore.

D. when you get your hair cut in a mohawk and you know you look good.

Answer: None of the above. It's fine to be proud of something you've done or happy about something you've gotten, but you're going to lose friends in a hurry if you talk about yourself all the time as if you're better than everybody. If you've got good news, share it—once. (More than once means it's not news anymore.) If you look good, people can see that for themselves. And if you know a secret, it's not going to be a secret for long if you blab it!

When someone you don't know very well asks how you are, . . .

A. answer honestly. Tell all about having the flu, including how green your snot was and how many times you barfed.

B. even if you're just feeling ordinary, say you're doing just *fabulous!* Lie about getting a pony, earning straight As, and having a secret admirer.

C. don't answer. This person could be an alien spy plotting to take over the world. Don't give out any information!

D. answer "Fine, thanks. How are you?"

Answer: D. If you've been sick, your pals might actually want to hear all the gory details. And if a parent or a doctor asks how you are, of course you should tell the whole yucky truth. But most people would rather not know the color of your snot or the duration of your barf-o-rama (or hear a boring speech about how great you are). When people you don't know ask how you are, they're really saying "I hope you're well." You don't need to fill them in on exactly how you're doing, make up stuff, or worry about evil aliens. By replying "Fine, thanks. How are you?" you're saying "Thanks for wishing me well. I hope you're well, too."

Family Matters

One of the best things about being at home is that you can do things there that you might not want to do in public. Snack on dill pickles with maple syrup. Watch TV in your pajamas all day. But it's also easy to forget your manners at home, around the people you know best: your family. A little dab of thoughtfulness will show your family how much you care about them. (And I'm sure you do care about them, even if you won't admit it!)

When you take your clothes off, . . .

A. put them in the laundry hamper, bag, basket, or chute unless they're not dirty or stinky.

B. crumple them up on top of your dresser to keep it from getting dusty.

C. drape them over your chair to air out. Maybe you'll be able to wear them again tomorrow.

D. leave them on the floor or wherever you feel like dropping them. The Laundry Fairy will whisk them away and bring them back magically clean.

Answer: A. Dirty clothes can get really stinky if they lie around too long or if you wear them over and over again. (Euuww!) If you answered D, I have news for you: The Laundry Fairy has retired and is now scuba diving in Florida.

When you take a shower or bath, . . .

A. be sure to leave evidence. Splash water all over the bathroom and leave dirt and hair stuck to the soap.

B. wash all over, clean up after yourself, and let a parent know when supplies run low.

C. wash only what looks dirty. Don't bother washing any body parts that were covered by clothes.

D. hide the shampoo, then enjoy watching your dripping-wet brother run around the house in a towel looking for it.

Answer: B. If you only wash what looks dirty when you bathe or shower, it won't be long before you're a slimy, stinky scuzzball. (Your family will love you anyway, but they sure won't want to get close to you!) Your body sweats all over and collects germs that you can't see, so it's wise to give it a good scrub regularly. Don't worry about leaving evidence; everyone can tell whether you've bathed just by smelling you. As for hiding the shampoo . . . I don't advise playing bathroom pranks on your siblings for one very good reason: wet towels really hurt when they're used as weapons!

After you brush your teeth, you should . . .

A. place the uncapped toothpaste tube on the floor right inside the bathroom door. Then laugh like a hyena when someone steps on it and toothpaste squirts all over!

B. see how many objects you can stick to the wall using toothpaste as glue.

C. put the cap back on the toothpaste tube and wipe up any blobs of toothpaste or spit you've left behind.

D. use toothpaste to write "Mom is the coolest!" on the bathroom mirror.

Answer: C. Telling your mom you think she's cool is a great idea, but I don't recommend the Colgate-on-mirror method. It may make your mom smile for a nanosecond, but then she'll hand you a rag . . . and you'll be stuck scrubbing away your love note (along with any brownie points you were hoping to gain). In fact, I don't recommend leaving toothpaste anywhere but in a tightly capped tube. Don't you just want to gag when you find blobs of goo stuck to things in the bathroom? If you hate it when others forget to clean up after themselves, start a Stamp Out Bathroom Goo crusade by setting a good example.

If you want to go into a room at home, but the door is closed, . . .

A. light a string of firecrackers under the door to blast it open, then go in.

B. knock first and wait for someone to yell "Come in!" or open the door.

C. open the door quietly and peek in. This is a great way to find out secret stuff useful for teasing and blackmail.

D. barge right in. Someone might be sneaking cookies, and you don't want to miss out.

Answer: B. Let's pretend for a moment that you're on the other side of the door. Let's say you're in your underwear . . . or hiding your secret diary . . . or telling a friend that you have a crush on your gym teacher . . . or going to the bathroom. How would you feel if someone snooped or barged in on you or blasted the door off its hinges? Family members do need to share a lot in order to get along, but it's also important that they don't share EVERYTHING. (I mean, who really wants to see their siblings in their underwear anyway? Gross!) Everyone needs some time alone.

Standing between the TV and someone who's watching it . . .

A. is a great way to get someone's attention.

B. isn't too bright, unless you've learned to duck quickly.

C. is a very effective way to annoy a sibling.

D. is inconsiderate.

Answers: B, C, and D. *A is wrong because standing in front of the TV is actually a DANGEROUS way to get someone's attention! You know those little pillows on the couch? They're called "throw pillows" for a reason, and they're usually about as soft as a soccer ball. If you simply must stand in front of the TV, you'd better sharpen up your dodge-ball skills. Better yet, remember that you're not made of glass . . . so don't be a "pane."*

When you spill milk on the kitchen floor, the best thing to do is . . .

A. add some chocolate syrup for flavor, then lick it up.

B. give a blood-curdling scream and tell your parents a big rat just ran by, scaring you and making you spill.

C. run away from home. When the police find you eighty miles away the next night, your folks will be so glad to see you that they'll forget about the Milk Disaster.

D. wipe it up with a paper towel or a rag.

Answer: D. You might feel like an idiot when you miss your cereal bowl and pour milk on the kitchen floor, but don't get your undies in a bunch. Everybody makes silly, klutzy mistakes now and then. (Tip: Ask your parents to tell you about their big blunders. You'll feel much better when you hear about the dorky things THEY'VE done!) When you goof up accidentally, just laugh at yourself and apologize to anyone your mistake might have affected, then fix it . . . and forget it.

When you use the last bit of butter from the Jumbo Tub o' Gold, you should . . .

A. fill the tub with fishing bait and put it back in the fridge. Worms and grubs last longer if you keep 'em cold!

B. stash the goopy tub under the couch for a couple of weeks. Soon you'll have a cool collection of mold for science class.

C. rinse the tub and toss it in the recycling or garbage bin, then let your parents know that you're out of butter.

D. use the tub to mix up a little of everything in the kitchen, then see if you can get anyone to eat your creation.

Answer: C. If you get your parents' permission and follow their safety rules, there's nothing wrong with creative cooking. But use a sturdy bowl, not a flimsy butter tub. And don't expect anyone to try stuff you wouldn't eat yourself. (Chocolate-chip-and-cabbage omelets, anyone?) It's fine to use an old butter tub for storage, but label it so no one winds up eating stinkworms on toast for breakfast. If you're going to grow mold, keep it somewhere out of the way. You don't want to get stuck cleaning up after your pet when it decides to eat your science project!

On a family road trip, . . .

A. drink lots and try to set a record for Peeing in the Most Rest Stops on One Trip.

B. help the driver stay awake by playing the radio full blast on KAZU, the all-kazoo, all-the-time radio station.

C. show your road-trip spirit by asking "Are we there yet?" every five minutes.

D. entertain everyone with a skit called Noises I Can Make with My Armpits.

Answer: None of the above. Each of these answers is like a mad scientist's invention: there's a good idea in there somewhere, but it's all twisted! It's wise to bring stuff to drink in the car so you don't have to stop whenever you get thirsty. Helping the driver stay awake, showing your family spirit, and entertaining everyone are nice ideas, too. But use your noodle and try not to do things that are just going to make everyone cranky. I'm sure your family would never think of ditching you in a rest stop, but why tempt them?

When your parents say they're dreading Aunt Helen's upcoming visit, you should . . .

A. tell Aunt Helen when she arrives. She'll probably bake you a cake to thank you.

B. agree loudly. Say you think Aunt Helen smells like yak poop, and you'd rather burn down the house than let her visit.

C. keep your new knowledge to yourself.

D. call Aunt Helen and tell her that your pet tarantulas escaped from their tank today, and you haven't found them all yet.

Answer: C. If Aunt Helen thinks there are huge, hairy spiders on the loose in your house, she might stay away . . . for a while. But the truth will come out eventually, and when it does, you'll wish you were a spider so you could skitter away and hide from your parents' wrath. The same goes for telling Aunt Helen what your parents say. Family feuds can start when folks with loose lips and hollow heads make, repeat, or act on negative comments. So keep your yak-poop thoughts to yourself and remember: The great thing about families is that they'll stand by you no matter what you smell like!

Your dad's journal, your mom's mail, and your sister's e-mail . . .

A. are none of your business.

B. make handy, funny, and educational reading material.

C. will give you great ideas for stories to write in English class.

D. are the only places to find out The Truth about Your Family.

Answer: A. I suppose it's POSSIBLE that your dad was raised by wolves or that your sister is really an undercover FBI agent. But the odds against it are so great, it's not worth risking your neck to read their private stuff and find out for sure. (Remember how tough a noogie your sister can give?) Everybody has a right to privacy, and every decent person respects the privacy of others.

Social Graces

Sure, it's easy to get away with the occasional burp or fart when you're in your own house. Your family loves you no matter what. (And with perfect timing, those "slips" in manners may become family legends!) But remember that it's a little different out in public. You only get one chance to make a good first impression with the new people you meet each day.

When you open a door that closes by itself, hold the door open . . .

A. until the person behind you walks through or can get a hand on it.

B. until you see someone coming, then slam it shut. See how many people you can knock over before someone calls the cops.

C. long enough to let all those poor cold flies in where it's safe and warm.

D. only for people who look rich. They might give you money for being so polite.

Answer: A. *If you let a bunch of flies indoors, they'll wind up buzzing around your head all day and landing on your lunch. (Gag! Think about the crud flies walk around on!) And although a game of Door Slam might be fun while it lasts, I guarantee that you won't enjoy spending the night in the slammer. Don't waste your time waiting around for rich people to reward you for holding the door open. Folks who are that rich have their own servants to do such stuff. Just hold a door open until someone right behind you can get a hand on it. If the person seems to need a little extra help—a small child, an old or sick person, or someone carrying packages—hold the door open until the person walks through. The grateful smile you'll get will make you glad you did!*

You're waiting to see the doctor, and a woman across the room has a disgusting rash on her face. You should . . .

A. run over and examine the rash up close, because you might be a doctor someday.

B. mind your own business. Don't stare at the rash or say anything about it.

C. elbow your little brother and say "If you touch my comic books again, I'm gonna have that lady come over and rub her face all over yours so your head rots off."

D. tiptoe over to the woman and whisper "Excuse me, ma'am, but I couldn't help noticing that your rash looks just like the one on my baby sister's butt."

Answer: B. If you were at the doctor to get help for an uncomfortable problem—let's say an eraser is stuck up your nose—wouldn't it make you feel a million times worse if people were staring, pointing, teasing, or otherwise calling attention to you? Try to remember that the next time you see someone who looks or acts unlike what you're used to. People come in many kinds of packages, but we all have the same feelings inside, and we all deserve to be treated with kindness.

Give up your seat on a crowded bus or train . . .

A. if you discover that you've sat in a puddle.

B. only when you get to your stop.

C. for any fat old man. He could be Santa Claus traveling in disguise.

D. for anyone who might have trouble walking or standing.

Answer: A and D. Old people, people with disabilities, people carrying lots of packages or traveling with small children, and pregnant women are all folks who might need your seat—unless, of course, there's a puddle on it. In that case, no one wants it!

A kid is standing next to you on the bus, and you notice his zipper is open. You should . . .

A. make some spitballs and use the open fly for target practice.

B. start singing the Alphabet Song and belt out the "XYZ" part as a hint to "x-amine your zipper."

C. moo and oink and make other farm-animal sounds, then say "Hey, cowboy, your barn door is open."

D. ignore it or say quietly "Can I offer you my seat? And by the way, your fly's open."

Answer: D. Everyone goofs up getting dressed sometimes. When you're sleepy or late or worried about a pimple sprouting on the end of your nose, it's easy to forget your zipper, button your shirt crooked, or wear mismatched shoes. If you can tell a kid about his zipper problem calmly and quietly, go right ahead. You'll be doing him a favor. But if you can't do so without making a scene, do EVERYONE a favor and skip it. Would you want the whole bus to know if YOUR zipper were at half-mast?

When you've finished drinking juice from a single-serving bottle, . . .

A. imprison a toad in it along with a note that reads "Pucker up—I'm a prince!"

B. throw the bottle and lid separately into the nearest body of water. They'll sink to the bottom, where no one can see them.

C. screw the lid back on the bottle and hang on to it until you can toss it in a recycling bin or trash can.

D. invite all your friends to share the fun as you throw the bottle against a rock and watch it shatter into a zillion pieces.

__Answer: C.__ B and D are only for creepy litterbugs, and I'm sure you already know how uncool it is to litter. Be a friend to the earth—and to earth's critters, as well. If that toad in answer A really does turn out to be a prince, you're going to be in big trouble for locking him up in a sticky, sloppy old juice bottle!

To avoid boredom at the grocery store, . . .

A. hide in an empty cashier station and tell jokes over the loudspeaker.

B. slip stuff like Ex-Lax and pickled pigs' feet into people's carts, then hang around the checkout area and enjoy the confusion.

C. see how many free samples you can eat before you (1) puke or (2) get kicked out.

D. carry a book or a hand-held game and read or play while your parents shop.

Answer: D. It may seem as if adults drag kids to grocery stores just to torture them, but believe it or not, your parents probably dread shopping as much as you do. The less you bug them—and everyone else at the store—the quicker they'll get the job done, and you can all get out of there!

When you bring a boom box to the beach, . . .

A. sneak up on dozing sunbathers, then turn it on full-blast. Enjoy all the different ways people jump and yell when they're startled.

B. play it loudly enough for you to hear, but quietly enough to avoid bothering others.

C. keep the lifeguards alert by playing the *Jaws* soundtrack over and over.

D. crank it up whenever a good song comes on the radio. I mean, who wouldn't love to hear the Flaming Fleas' latest hit?

Answer: B. *Scaring the daylights out of sleeping sunbathers could be very entertaining, but be sure to consider all their possible reactions—which might include not only jumping and yelling but also clobbering you! As for playing the* Jaws *soundtrack . . . that would probably only tempt everyone at the beach to throw you to the sharks. And before you crank up the volume for any song, imagine that someone else has control of the boom box and just LOVES the Electric Polka Pumpers. Get the picture?*

Which of these questions is okay to ask?

A. "Holy smokes—how much do you weigh?"

B. "How much money do you make?"

C. "Why doesn't your family live together?"

D. "Didn't you used to be bald?"

*Answer: **None of the above.** It's true that there's no such thing as a stupid question. . . . After all, how can you learn anything if you never ask questions? But beware of asking about really personal stuff like someone's body, age, money, or relationships. Even if your curiosity is killing you. Even if you're truly concerned. Personal stuff can sometimes be embarrassing or painful, so it's best not to pry. If people want to talk about their personal stuff, they'll bring it up themselves.*

When you bump someone accidentally, you should . . .

A. go directly to the hospital. The person you bumped might have mad cow disease!

B. follow up by stomping on the person's foot. If you're going to hurt someone, do a thorough job of it.

C. say "Excuse me" using a tone of voice and an expression that show you really are sorry.

D. start humming a disco tune and dancing The Bump to cover up your klutziness.

Answer: C. Believe me: Humming disco music while dancing The Bump looks MUCH stupider than being a klutz. Everyone is klutzy sometimes, so if you accidentally bump someone, the person probably won't get mad—or even think twice about it—as long as you apologize. So don't have a cow. And don't worry about getting mad cow disease, either. You can't catch it—or just about any disease, for that matter—by bumping someone. And anyway, you're not a cow. (Are you?)

An expert skateboarder always . . .

A. skates in a way that endangers no one including him- or herself.

B. stays on the skateboard, even if it means running over an old fogey who can't get out of the way fast enough.

C. wears a helmet when skating indoors, where there are walls and furniture to crash into.

D. skates. Walking is for geeks!

Answer: A. Well, it's true that practice makes perfect; so the more you skate, the better you'll get. But if you skate like a maniac, you could be declared a public health hazard and forbidden to skate at all. Or you could hurt yourself badly enough that you'll NEVER become an expert. The next time you have an urge to skate down the stairs, imagine what might happen if your skateboard were to get snagged, sending you flying toward the nearest wall. Ever seen a bug smashed on a car windshield?

You want to ride the Octopus, but there's a really long line. What should you do?

A. Hide nearby and scream bloody murder. When everyone in line comes running to find out what's wrong, sneak over to the Octopus and hop on!

B. Go to the end of the line and pass the time chatting or daydreaming.

C. Eat a chili dog with sauerkraut while you wait in line. The gas you pass should scare away a couple dozen people.

D. Get in line and try to pass two people every time it moves. Before you know it, you'll be at the front!

Answer: B. Oooh, don't you just hate it when someone butts into line in front of you? It's so unfair—especially when you've been waiting patiently and trying to be nice. I bet you feel like tying that buttinski to the roller-coaster track! I'm sure YOU'D never dream of actually doing anything that naughty, but you can't predict what other folks might do when they're really steamed. Keep that in mind if you're ever tempted to trick your way to the front of a long line.

When you want to borrow something, . . .

A. tickle the person holding it, so he or she will drop it.

B. say that you hear it ticking. The person it belongs to will think it's a bomb and will want to get rid of it fast!

C. sing "Oh, I wish I were an Oscar Meyer wiener . . ." off-key at the top of your lungs until the owner hands over what you want just to shut you up.

D. ask before borrowing it, take good care of it, and return it soon.

Answer: D. Most people are glad to lend their possessions and share the fun, unless the item is in use or is really valuable or breakable. People might also refuse you if you're being a pain in the neck or acting like a lunatic. If you just ask nicely and return things promptly and in good condition, people will know you're responsible (not to mention sane), and you shouldn't have any trouble at all.

After saying "Ted looks even dorkier than usual in his new glasses," you realize Ted's standing behind you. What do you say?

A. "Um . . . I knew you were there. I was just seeing if you were listening."

B. "Now that you know how dorky you look, are you gonna get some better glasses?"

C. Nothing—you just wiggle your ears and disappear.

D. "Oh, wow, Ted, I'm sorry. That was a creepy thing to say, and I'm sorry I hurt your feelings."

Answer: D. C is what most people would wish for in this situation. But the ear-wiggling strategy has never been proven to work, so I'm afraid you're stuck. You have to say SOMETHING. Now, Ted may look dorky, but he's no dummy; he's not going to fall for A. And I don't recommend B either; it'll only get you into even more hot water. Just think about how you'd feel if you were in Ted's shoes and apologize. Or better yet, don't say mean things in the first place. Then you can be sure you'll never find yourself face-to-face with someone whose feelings you've hurt.

Euuww— Gross!

Some people don't like to be reminded of the perfectly natural sounds, smells, and goo that their bodies produce. If you're one of those people, don't be a wimp and skip this chapter. Manners apply to body functions, too! A lot of our bodily by-products contain invisible germs that can make other people sick. This chapter will show you how good manners can help you stay clean and keep your natural (but icky) body goo from bothering others.

When you sneeze, . . .

A. try to keep your eyes open. It's supposed to be impossible, so you'll be famous if you can do it.

B. cover your nose and mouth with a tissue.

C. spray as many people as you can, so you'll have lots of company staying home sick with you.

D. cover your mouth and nose with your hand, then wipe your hand on anything convenient: your shirt, your sister's ponytail, the family dog . . . whatever.

Answer: B. If you let your germs make other people sick, they'll be downright cranky with you and not very good company at all. So save the energy it takes to spray your germs all over the place. Sneeze into a tissue instead; it's the best way to keep your spit and snot to yourself. Sneezes do have a way of sneaking up on people, so you might not always have time to reach for a tissue. In that case, cover your mouth and nose with your hand and wash your hands right away. As for trying to keep your eyes open while you sneeze . . . If you manage it, you may indeed become famous: for being the only person in history whose eyeballs popped out!

If you're with someone who sneezes, . . .

A. yell "Incoming!" and duck to avoid flying snot, spit, and other fallout.

B. cough back in reply.

C. say "God bless you" or "Gesundheit."

D. offer the person a tissue—even if you've already used it.

Answer: C. Let's assume that the somebody you're with is a human, not a gorilla. Gorillas are not known for their delightful manners, but most humans are civilized enough not to sneeze right in other people's faces. So it's probably not necessary to hit the dirt. Let's also assume that YOU'RE not a gorilla, so coughing back isn't an option, either. Any sneezer would be grateful for a clean tissue, but don't make him or her even sicker by offering a tissue that's already full of goop. A simple "God bless you" or "Gesundheit" (German for "health") will do the trick.

If your nose starts running during a meal, the best thing to wipe it on is . . .

A. the tablecloth—it's nice and big.

B. your sleeve—it's always handy.

C. a hanky or tissue. If you don't have one, go get one.

D. Why bother wiping it? Just sniffle or let it run!

Answer: C. Even if you're SURE the tablecloth would look cool decorated with your snot, and you feel you MUST try it or you'll suffocate your creativity, don't! If you wipe your nose on the tablecloth (or your sleeve or arm or hand or anything but a hanky or tissue), you could gross out the other people at the table so much that they throw up all over you. Then you'd have more than just a runny nose to worry about. Snot (not to mention vomit) is full of germs. Keep your germs to yourself, and everyone else'll do the same.

Nose picking . . .

A. should be done only in private.

B. is exciting—you never know what you'll find!

C. is a great way to find stuff to fling at your friends in class. Pick it, lick it, stick it, flick it!

D. is an excellent exercise for budding archeologists.

Answer: A. Let's face it: Noses create crud, and sometimes you've just got to do something about crud buildup. But nobody wants to see you digging into your nose. And nobody wants to see what you dig out of your nose, either—unless it's a free ticket to Disney World—and what are the odds of finding THAT in there?

When you yawn, . . .

A. open your mouth as wide as you can, so everyone can admire your terrific teeth.

B. enhance your yawning experience by stretching and making loud cat noises.

C. put your gaping mouth to work doing something useful like catching bugs.

D. cover your mouth.

Answer: D. You can't spread germs just by opening your mouth, but that's not the reason you should cover it when you yawn. This is: Many people are grossed out by the sight of other people's tonsils and spit and chewed-up food. . . . In fact, I'm feeling queasy just thinking about it. And if you're going to stretch and meow and act like a cat when you yawn, perhaps you should also be eating kitty chow and using a litter box!

Which of the choices below is okay to do?

A. You neatly scoop some dip onto a chip, take a small bite, then scoop more dip onto the rest of the chip and finish it.

B. After tasting your oatmeal, you decide it needs sugar. You scoop some from the sugar bowl with your wet spoon.

C. You can't finish all your peas, but you don't want to waste food, so you put your uneaten peas back in the serving bowl.

D. You want more punch, but you can't find the ladle, so you dip some out with your used cup instead.

*Answer: **None of the above.** All of these choices fall into the category of Slobbering, which is definitely not okay. Note: Take care not to confuse Slobbering (sharing unwanted saliva) with the related category Authorized Spit Swapping (smooching with permission).*

When you feel you're going to burp, . . .

A. hold it in, even if it makes your belly explode.

B. do it as quietly as you can. Close and cover your mouth, then say "Excuse me."

C. announce it proudly. Stand on a chair and say "Attention, please! Everybody freeze! Da-dum-da-dum-dum-dum: *BURP!*"

D. try to say "Yabba-dabba-doo!" as you burp.

Answer: B. *Just as everyone's nose creates crud, everyone's tummy creates gas. And the body has to get rid of gas to keep from bursting. So that means that everyone burps and everyone (yes, everyone) farts. Big and little, old and young, male and female, ordinary and important. Even the President of the United States. It's no big deal—unless you MAKE a big deal of it. When you need to get rid of a tummy bubble, just try not to gross people out. And if you think anyone has heard (or smelled) it, say "Excuse me."*

When should you wash your hands?

A. Every five minutes. Germs are everywhere, so you can't be too careful!

B. Never. Germs are everywhere (even in water), so you can't be too careful!

C. Only when they're so sticky that you can't pry them apart after clapping.

D. whenever they're dirty, before you eat or prepare food, after you use the bathroom, and often when you're sick.

Answer: D. Long ago, it was common for people to get really horrible diseases. Their skin rotted off (ugh!); their limbs turned black (euuww!); and they coughed up their lungs (blech!). But most of the nasty ills people used to get are extremely rare now. Why? Somewhere along the way, people figured out that they could stay pretty healthy by staying clean. Disease-causing germs hate clean bodies. You don't need to wash your hands every five minutes (another good way to lose your skin), but do scrub 'em whenever they're grungy, before handling food, after using the bathroom, and often when you're sick. You'll be doing yourself—and all humankind—a big favor.

If you get an itch in a private place, . . .

A. scratch it immediately. *Ahhhhh.*

B. ignore it if it's not too bad. It may go away if you think about something else.

C. excuse yourself to someplace where you can be alone and then scratch.

D. try to scratch without looking as if you're scratching. Wiggle around in your seat or rub against a tree. Be creative!

Answer: B or C. *Reaching for your private parts in public is sure to embarrass you and anyone else unlucky enough to be nearby—so avoid A. Scratch privately or don't scratch at all. Sneaky scratching (answer D) may indeed keep people from figuring out that you have an embarrassing itch—but it's also likely to make them think you have other problems!*

When you go to the bathroom, . . .

A. turn on the faucet or whistle loudly to drown out the noises your body makes.

B. leave the door open and play Name that Noise with whoever else is around.

C. close the door.

D. leave the door open in case you do anything stinky.

Answer: C. You can't go wrong if you simply follow the Golden Toilet Rule: Peeing and Pooping Shall Be Private Endeavors for Everyone over the Age of Three. So if someone has to use the toilet, that person should keep the experience to him- or herself. (No sharing sounds or smells on purpose!) And others should ignore the fact that someone's using the toilet. (No joking, snickering, face-making, or nose-holding!)

Table Talk

It's not always easy to remember good table manners—especially when you're hungrier than a bear at the end of winter. But unless you've spent the past few months hibernating in a cave, you probably don't have a very good excuse for acting like an animal. Follow the table-manners tips in this chapter to make sure that no one mistakes you for a horrible, hungry beast.

The dinner table is a great place for . . .

A. talking with your family.

B. artistic adventures. Try ketchup painting, mashed-potato sculpture, bean music, and dinner-table drama. (How many peas can *you* stuff up your nose?)

C. making faces at your siblings. See if you can get away with showing them your chewed-up food, too.

D. yakking on the phone.

Answer: A. For many families, dinner is the only time everyone's in the same room at once. That's why the dinner table is a great place to fill everyone in on your day and catch up on the latest family news. If you're yakking on the phone, you might miss something important—like the vote for this year's family vacation—and wind up spending two weeks in Hooterville, Saskatchewan. I don't recommend making faces or doing anything peculiar with your food. Even if someone laughs at your antics, remember that those who laugh while eating or drinking tend to squirt stuff out their noses . . . and you're right in the line of fire.

When you want more French fries, and the bowl is at the other end of the table, . . .

A. reach or climb across the table and grab them before they disappear.

B. grunt "Mmff! Mmff!" through a mouthful of food to get everyone's attention, then point to the fries.

C. swallow anything in your mouth, wait for a break in conversation, then say "Please pass the French fries."

D. shout "Fling me some fries, wouldja?"— even if your mouth is full.

Answer: C. Very few French fries have magical powers, so they're not likely to vanish into thin air if you don't grab them fast enough. You won't go hungry if you just take a minute to swallow whatever you're eating and ask for the fries politely. If you try D with a mouthful of food, that food could wind up flying out of your mouth onto other people's plates. Then they may very well fling the desired fries at you—but perhaps a little harder than you'd like!

If you need to go to the bathroom during a meal, . . .

A. squirm, pass gas, or make faces until someone asks you to leave the table.

B. say "May I be excused for a minute?"

C. jump out of your chair and yell "Pardon me! Gotta pee!"

D. just go right there in your chair. It's rude to get up in the middle of a meal.

Answer: B. *If you answered anything else (especially D—gag!), please refer to page 60 and brush up on the Golden Toilet Rule. It's okay to get up in the middle of a meal if you have a good reason. For example, if your house is burning down, if your dog is gnawing on the mail carrier's leg, or if you really need to go to the bathroom . . . by all means, get up! When leaving a meal to go to the bathroom, it's best not to make a big deal out of it. Just excuse yourself politely.*

When milk is served with a meal, . . .

A. grab a straw and show your baby brother how to blow bubbles through it.

B. have a contest to see who can get the biggest milk mustache. Award bonus points for milk beards and milk eyebrows.

C. try to make your sister laugh, so milk squirts out her nose.

D. remember to wipe your mouth after drinking.

*Answer: **D.** Milk manners are simple: Milk is strictly for drinking—not bubbling, wearing, squirting, or any other creative verbs.*

If you drop your napkin on the floor, . . .

A. you can slip your liver and onions to the dog while you pick up the napkin.

B. wipe your mouth and hands on your clothes, or just lick your lips and fingers clean.

C. pick it up and keep using it. So what if it's been on the floor?

D. say "I'm sorry; I dropped my napkin. May I have a clean one?"

Answer: D. *I don't advise using a napkin that's been on the floor. Who knows what kind of germ-filled crud it might have picked up? You will need a napkin to finish the meal, though (unless you're trying to prove you're actually an ape), so just ask for a clean one. As for slipping your dinner to the dog . . . skip it. Everyone's going to notice Fido's liver-and-onion breath, so you won't get away with that trick for long.*

Forks . . .

A. are fun! Plant hundreds of plastic forks in your neighbors' yard at night, then enjoy their shouts of delight in the morning.

B. are HUGE in Grand Forks, North Dakota, so avoid eating in that city unless your mouth is really big.

C. should be used for eating most foods.

D. don't hold peas very well, so always mash your peas before eating them.

Answer: C. Answer A might land you in jail for vandalism. If you believe B, you might also want to stay away from Ugley, England, and Black Butt, Australia. As for D . . . People have indeed been chasing peas around their plates for centuries. But peas—and other roly-poly, wiggly, or slippery foods—can be forked up easily if you know the trick. Just use your fork to push the problem food against the side of your plate or your knife, and you'll have no trouble at all scooping it into your mouth.

Which of the following are finger foods?

A. Mashed potatoes with gravy

B. Raw carrots and celery

C. Chicken-noodle soup

D. All six-legged creatures

Answer: B. If you're under the age of two or you're a chimpanzee, all of the choices above could be finger foods. But if you're reading this book, you're neither a baby nor a chimp. So listen up, because sometimes it's tricky to figure out how you should pick up your food. Here are a few pointers: (1) Most snacks are finger foods, so if you see a bowl or plate of food like olives, nuts, chips, cookies, pretzels, or cheese and crackers with no forks in sight, it's safe to assume you're looking at finger food. (2) If you're at a picnic or a family meal that's not fancy, you can use your fingers to eat food like chicken, bacon, ribs, corn on the cob, pizza, shrimp cocktail, fish sticks, pickles, raw vegetables, fruit, French fries, tacos, and sandwiches. (3) If all else fails and you're not sure of how to eat something, just wait for others to start eating first, then follow their lead.

When a dish is passed to you and there's no serving utensil with it, . . .

A. ask where the serving utensil is. If someone has accidentally begun eating with it, fetch a clean one.

B. carefully lick off your own fork and use that to serve yourself.

C. just use your fingers.

D. stick your face into the food, gobble up as much as you want, and pass the dish along.

Answer: A. When you're really hungry or you're busy telling a great joke,* it's easy to do goofy, absent-minded things like eating with a giant serving spoon. So don't make a stink if someone else at the table does that—it might be you next time! Sticking your licked-off fork, your face, or your fingers into the dish isn't the solution either—that's slobbering. Just get up and grab a new serving utensil.

* Q: What did the fish say when it hit its head?
  A: "Dam!"

If you bite into some gristle, bone, or any-thing odd while chewing your food, . . .

A. make barfing noises and spew the whole mouthful onto your plate.

B. use it to practice your spitball aim. Try to hit the person across the table right between the eyes.

C. quietly remove it from your mouth and set it on your plate or spit it into a paper napkin.

D. call 911 right away, because obviously someone is trying to kill you.

Answer: C. Even if you're a vegetarian, you're bound to find weird things in your food every now and then. If it's not bone or gristle (that icky, rubbery stuff), it might be a pebble trying to pass itself off as a bean. No one expects you to swallow anything weird, but do try to get rid of it in a way that won't gross anyone out or hurt anyone's feelings.

It's okay to snag some cake from your brother's plate . . .

A. if you're bigger than he is.

B. when he owes you for not telling your parents what really happened with their toothbrushes and the toilet.

C. on Halloween, because if you're wearing a costume, he won't know it's you.

D. only if he says it's okay.

Answer: D. Even if you're bigger, older, or sneakier than your brother right now, don't forget that little siblings grow up. Sometimes, as a matter of fact, they grow quite big and clever. Most have good memories, too. It's better to be nice to them now than to have to plead for mercy later.

You're waiting for your food in a restaurant and notice salt, pepper, mustard, ketchup, sugar, and cream on the table. You should . . .

A. use the condiments to draw portraits of other diners—this'll help you pass the time and provide souvenirs for all.

B. loosen the tops of the salt and pepper shakers so they'll fall off when the next person uses them.

C. take a swig of ketchup, then scream "Auugghhh! I've been poisoned!" as you let it dribble out of your mouth like blood.

D. sneakily sprinkle sugar on someone's shoulders, then ask politely about his or her dandruff problem.

Answer: None of the above. If you try any of these messy, mean stunts in a restaurant, somebody's going to clobber you—and whoever does it will get a round of applause from everyone else.

Chewing with your mouth open . . .

A. is the only way to aerate your food properly.

B. can really kill someone else's appetite.

C. lets people see how delicious your food is.

D. is a good exercise to prevent lockjaw.

Answer: B. Answers A, C, and D may seem perfectly logical, but they're really just a bunch of baloney. Food doesn't need to be aerated while you chew it; the only way to prevent lockjaw is to get a tetanus shot; and chewed-up food looks disgusting, not delicious. If you want to gross out everyone else at the table so there'll be more food for you, chewing with your mouth open is a good plan. But be aware that it might get you grounded!

You should help clear the table . . .

A. unless it's someone else's turn according to the family chore schedule, or you're in a restaurant.

B. right away when you smell a stinky odor—like limburger cheese or lutefisk—coming from the kitchen.

C. as soon as you're done eating, so you can go play. Grab food out of people's mouths if you have to.

D. whenever you eat at a restaurant. Maybe the server will share the tip with you!

Answer: **A.** *I've heard that limburger cheese tastes like sweaty socks—and why anyone would want to eat lutefisk (fish soaked in lye, a liquid made from wood ashes) is beyond me. But you never know . . . You might actually like these dishes—or other stinky, unusual foods. Lots of people do. So give them a chance before you clear the table and hide in the closet. I'm confident that you know better than to grab food from others, so I won't bother to explain why you shouldn't. As for trying to nab a bit of someone's tip . . . Skip it. If a server has worked hard to provide you with a nice meal, he or she deserves every penny of that tip!*

Helping Others Feel at Home

Having guests at your home can be a lot of fun. It can also be challenging, so when you're a host, you'll need to be even more kind and patient than you usually are. The good part about being a great host is that you'll get the same VIP treatment when you visit your guests' homes. This chapter will show you how to make all your guests want to come back—and treat you like royalty when you visit them.

When a parent has company, . . .

A. run and hide—someone might want to kiss you!

B. impress everyone by showing off your collection of bellybutton lint.

C. say hello, then go back to whatever you were doing.

D. liven things up by streaking through the room without clothes on.

*Answer: **C.** When a parent has company, the guests will surely want to meet you—or say hi if they already know you. So if you find yourself in the same room with the adults, be friendly and greet the guests. But remember that they've come to visit with your parent, not you. If you lurk about or take up too much of their time showing off your lint collection (or your birthday suit), they won't have a chance to talk about what a delightful kid you are.*

Your parent's guests have brought their son, Jack, with them. What should you do?

A. Ignore him; he might have cooties.

B. Play hide-and-seek, and tell Jack he's it. While he counts, run off to play at a neighbor's house.

C. Practice your kickboxing moves on him.

D. Ask Jack what he likes to do. If possible, do that. If not, suggest a favorite game of yours.

Answer: D. If Jack had cooties, his parents wouldn't bring him anywhere, so don't worry about that. Jack probably feels as awkward about being dragged along on this visit as you do about having a kid you don't know in the house. You can make everyone— including yourself—more comfortable by simply being friendly. Who knows . . . you might discover that you have something in common and wind up with a new pal! At the very least, you'll enjoy yourself while Jack's around instead of worrying about avoiding him—and getting in trouble for it later.

Your friend Meg is visiting you, and you agree to play a game. How do you decide who goes first?

A. Have a spitting contest. Whoever can hawk the biggest goober gets to go first.

B. Meg is your guest, so you let her go first.

C. Give Meg a noogie until she shouts "Okay! Okay! You go first!"

D. Sock Meg in the stomach. While she's catching her breath, you start the game.

Answer: B. *If you give your friends noogies or sock them in the gut every time you want to play a game, you won't have friends for long. The easiest way to start a game is simply to let whoever's the guest go first. If you're the host this time, your turn to be the guest will come soon enough. When there's more than one guest, or you're not at anybody's home, a quick, simple contest is a good way to decide who goes first. But no goober-hawking, please. (Only pro baseball players are allowed to spit in public.) Try rolling some dice or playing Rock-Paper-Scissors instead.*

At your birthday party, you get to . . .

A. play whatever games you want. Now's your chance to play Truth or Dare and make your sister tell you whom she has a crush on—or make her eat a dustbunny!

B. have the first piece of birthday cake.

C. throw food at whomever you choose— even your parents!

D. keep anything your guests bring with them. This is a great way to collect cool toys and clothes.

Answer: B. Yup, it's your privilege as the Birthday Boss to command the first slice of birthday cake. Enjoy! But take care not to push your birthday "rights" too far, or your guests will start calling you the Birthday Brat instead.

If someone gives you a gift that you hate at your birthday party, . . .

A. stick your tongue out at the giver when no one else is looking.

B. "accidentally" drop the gift in the punch bowl. If you ruin the stupid thing, you won't get stuck wearing or playing with it.

C. smile, say thanks sincerely, and try to mention one nice thing about the gift.

D. present the giver with a special party favor: a medal that reads "Goofiest Gift."

Answer: C. Goofy gifts are a fact of life. Who hasn't, at one time or another, opened a present and thought "What in the world am I going to do with THIS?" But even when you think a gift is stupendously stupid, you can't forget that it's still a gift. A gift is an outward sign of someone's desire to make you happy. And that alone is worth a big smile, an honest thank-you, and a few nice words.

You invite your new friend, Randy, to your house for the first time. When he rings the doorbell, you . . .

A. answer the door yourself and bring Randy to meet your family first thing.

B. for laughs, tell your hyperactive pit bull, Spaz, to "Sic 'im!" (Spaz looks scary, but you know he's really a softie.)

C. yell "Come in!" and let Randy wander through the house to find you.

D. bring Randy straight to the kitchen and whip up two peanut butter, egg, and orange juice power drinks. You'll need the energy for playing.

Answer: A. If you sic your dog on Randy (even as a joke) or make him wander like a lost puppy through your house, he may start wondering if you invited him over just to torture him. Your new friend could become a new enemy faster than you can say "Sic 'im!" Remember that Randy's in unfamiliar territory, and try to make him feel comfortable. If you answer the door yourself and introduce Randy to your family right away, you'll make sure the visit starts off on friendly footing.

There's only one little brownie left, and you're dying to eat it. Suddenly your best pal shows up. What do you do?

A. Shove the brownie in your mouth.

B. Point out the window and shout "Holy buckets—a six-legged squirrel!" While your pal tries to spot the mutant rodent, you gobble up the brownie.

C. Eat the brownie later, when you're alone.

D. Tell your pal that you saw your brother sneeze into the brownie batter.

Answer: C. Lying (answers B and D) is for dweebs, and answer A is only okay if you haven't eaten anything for a whole month. It'd be nice if you could share the brownie with your pal, but if it's really small, it's probably not worth splitting. Nothing's worse than a tiny, teasing taste of something delicious. (Except, perhaps, watching someone else eat something yummy while you stand there and drool.) So if you can't split the brownie and you don't want to give it away, either, spare yourself (and your pal) the agony and save it to eat later.

Good Guests Get Invited Back

Visiting other people's homes can sometimes be awkward. What if they have rules that are different from what you're used to? What if something embarrassing happens? This chapter will show you how to be a gracious guest no matter what, so your hosts will always welcome you back.

When you enter a friend's home and notice that it smells weird, you should . . .

A. keep your opinion to yourself.

B. smile and ask "Do you guys have a road-kill collection?"

C. request a clothespin for your nose.

D. ask "Does that horrible stink mean we're having hazardous waste for dinner?"

Answer: A. You may be the only person in the world who thinks your friend's home smells weird. But even if eighteen zillion people agree with you, telling your friend what you think of the stink will embarrass him or her and make you look like an oaf. Just concentrate on how much fun you're having to keep your mind off the smell.

When you're at a party in someone else's home, . . .

A. go on a mini scavenger hunt. Try to collect a postage stamp, a dead bug, a cotton swab, a hairball, and a penny minted before you were born.

B. sneak into the kitchen and mix coffee beans into the kitty chow.

C. have fun without making mischief.

D. call people who weren't invited and tell them what a blast you're having.

Answer: C. I'll admit that a highly caffeinated cat could be pretty darn funny, but it would probably also be very unhappy. And playing a prank like that will definitely ensure that your name is missing from future invitation lists. The same goes for snooping, stealing stuff, and abusing the phone. Try to make fun without making mischief. (Organize a game. Tell your best joke. Do your Donald Duck impression. Be creative.) And count yourself lucky to have been invited.

When you sit down for a meal at a friend's house, . . .

A. try to hang a spoon from your nose while you wait for everyone to get settled.

B. show your enthusiasm by banging your silverware on the table and cheering "Rub-a-dub-dub! Bring on the grub!"

C. inspect your silverware to make sure it's clean.

D. wait to dig in until everyone is seated and someone else starts eating.

Answer: D. Eating over at a friend's house is fun to do now and then. It's a great way to spend more time with your friend, try new foods, and get to know your friend's family better. Go ahead and feel proud that you've been invited to join your friend's family meal. In return for this kindness, you'll naturally want to be as nice as you can. Wait until all are seated and someone else starts eating so you don't accidentally wind up chomping food while the family says grace. And I'm sure you wouldn't dream of insulting or annoying them with the silverware stunts in answers A, B, and C.

You're at a friend's house for dinner, and someone offers you some salmon. You can't stand salmon. What do you do?

A. Politely say "No, thanks. Just looking at that fish makes my skin crawl."

B. Say "Thanks, but I don't care for any."

C. Scream. Stick out your tongue. Clutch your throat. Pretend to pass out.

D. Don't say anything; that would be rude. Force yourself to eat some salmon, then upchuck as quietly as you can.

Answer: B. For eons, adults have been making kids eat food they can't stand. I'm happy to announce that most of us now realize that wasn't very smart. (Believe it or not, adults make mistakes. Sometimes we even admit it!) All people—kids and adults alike—have personal tastes, and people should never feel forced to eat hated foods unless there's nothing else available. If someone offers you a food you can't stand, don't freak out. Just tell the truth: You don't care for any. Period. Skip the gory details and drama, which will only hurt people's feelings.

When your host passes around a plate of cookies, . . .

A. paw through them to find the biggest one.

B. take one, then slip another up your sleeve to snack on later.

C. pick up a cookie and sniff it to make sure it's not something nasty like a pickled-prune macaroon.

D. say "Thank you," take the first cookie you touch, and pass the plate along. If the cookies are a kind you don't like, just pass the plate without saying anything.

Answer: D. *Sure, it's always nice to have a spare cookie standing between you and starvation, but your host will think you're a pig if you take more than one right off the bat. (It's okay to take another cookie if your host OFFERS you seconds.) Should you choose to root around for the biggest cookie in the batch, you may as well oink while you're at it. The same goes for sniffing. If you can't tell what kind of cookies you're dealing with by looking at them, just ask!*

After a meal at someone else's home, . . .

A. thank your host for the great food and offer to help clear the table.

B. ask "Can we have pepperoni pizza next time?"

C. disappear into the bathroom long enough for someone else to do the dishes.

D. burp loudly and rub your belly to show your happiness.

Answer: A. After eating a meal at someone else's home, you can make your host's day by showing how happy and grateful you are. (Even if you were hoping for pepperoni pizza and got spinach soufflé, you would still be happy and grateful for your host's kindness.) A great way to do that is to give your host a big thank-you and offer to help with the cleanup. If you hide out in the bathroom too long, your host will think you're sick or see through your trick; either way, you'll hurt his or her feelings. And burping and belly-rubbing will just make you look like a slob, endangering your chances of getting invited back.

When you're at someone else's home and need to use the bathroom, . . .

A. do the pee-pee dance to hold it in.

B. say "I hafta wizz. Where's the can?"

C. ask "May I use your bathroom?" or "Could you please show me to your bathroom?"

D. stay away from tickling fingers and the sound of running water.

Answer: C. *Don't be embarrassed about having to go to the bathroom at someone else's house. Everybody has to go now and then, and no one expects you to hold it until you get home. If you try, you might end up wetting your pants—or worse: bursting your guts. (Now THAT would be really bad manners!) Just ask to use the bathroom nicely (using regular English, not slang), take care of business, and enjoy the rest of your visit.*

You always wear shoes in your house, but you're asked to remove them inside your friend's house. You . . .

A. say "No way—I might catch a fungus!"

B. do it.

C. demand at least three good reasons.

D. show the soles of your shoes to prove that there's no dog poop on them.

Answer: B. When you're in someone else's home, it's your duty as a guest to follow the house rules without making a stink about it. (Note: You can ditch this duty if you're asked to do anything you think is dangerous, bizarre, uncomfortable, or wrong. If that happens, firmly say no—and leave.) Removing your shoes is a perfectly safe and reasonable request, so just do it. Don't worry about foot fungus . . . If you use your noodle, you'll realize that you're being asked to shed your shoes because the floors are spotlessly clean!

Your mom has brought you along to visit her friends, the Dinkeldorfs. You're in the family room, and their cat, Dinky, throws up on the carpet in front of you. You . . .

A. wipe up the mess with the nearest throw pillow or blanket.

B. scream as if a vampire were sinking its fangs into your butt.

C. find the adults and say "Excuse me, but Dinky's been sick in the family room." Then let the Dinkeldorfs take care of it.

D. yell "Come quick! Dinky blew chunks all over the family room! It's all foamy with gray globs; I think he ate a lizard!"

Answer: C. It's okay to describe really yucky stuff when you're joking around with friends and trying to gross them out. But in any other situation, it's best to skip the disgusting details. If you're visiting someone else's house and the cat (or hamster or baby) throws up, or some other emergency happens, just let the adults know as quickly and calmly as you can.

The best way to avoid getting invited to old Aunt Edith's house is to . . .

A. torture her when she visits *your* house by dropping toy spiders on her head and teaching your dog to hide her cane.

B. interrupt her every three minutes to add to your story about the mating elephants you saw on TV.

C. tell her that head lice is going around at your school.

D. run around her house like a wild animal and gnaw on the furniture.

Answer: None of the above. Sorry, but you can't avoid visiting your relatives, so try to make the best of it. If you think Aunt Edith is just too boring or old or cranky to bother with, it could be because you haven't really tried to get to know her. She might surprise you by saying she used to fly stunt planes. Or show you a picture of herself at age twenty-three, wearing her Miss Ohio crown. Or tell you about the time she slipped a frog down her brother's shirt. Even if she does turn out to be a drag, remember that she's family, and part of being a family is caring for each other even when you'd rather be doing something else.

You're visiting your friend Tim, who has a swimming pool. You want to swim, but Tim wants to play with his new puppy. You . . .

A. push Tim in the pool.

B. say "I'm holding your puppy hostage. If you don't swim with me, you'll never see Spot again."

C. toss the puppy in the pool and shout "Look! Spot wants to swim, too!"

D. figure out some activity that both of you want to do.

Answer: D. *When you have your heart set on doing a certain activity, it can be hard to shift gears. But getting your way by bullying your friend isn't worth the price you might pay (namely, your friendship). If you're tempted to do something mean, remember that the main point of visiting your friend's house is to spend time with your friend—not his or her swimming pool or stereo or whatever. It only takes a little effort to figure out something you'll both enjoy doing. But it's a lot of hard work to patch up a broken friendship!*

You're having a snack at a friend's house, and your friend goes to the bathroom. While you're alone, you accidentally break a drinking glass. What should you do?

A. Pound on the bathroom door and yell "Help! I've had an accident!"

B. Find an adult and say "I've accidentally broken a drinking glass. I'm really sorry. How would you like me to clean it up?"

C. When your friend returns, say "Smooth move, Ex-Lax. Look what you knocked over when you rushed out of the room!"

D. Snatch up the broken glass, stuff it in the garbage, and don't tell anyone.

Answer: B. If you choose A, your friend's going to think you've either broken your arm or wet your pants. (Let him or her go to the bathroom in peace!) C is lying—an activity reserved for dweebs, as you'll recall)—and D is dangerous. Your friend's family deserves to know that they're one glass short and that there might be bits of broken glass lying about. Honesty is your best bet here (as always). Everyone is a klutz now and then, so no one's going to be mad at you when you reveal your little mishap.

When your host offers you a chocolate from a box of assorted chocolates, . . .

A. grab nine to make sure you get at least one you like.

B. choose one and eat it.

C. poke your finger into one after another until you find one that looks good.

D. take one and nibble the bottom of it. If you don't like it, put it back in the box.

Answer: B. Your host has offered you A chocolate, not nine or ten or even two, so touching (not to mention grabbing, poking, nibbling, or slobbering on) more than one would be greedy and rude. You're not going to keel over and die from eating one little chocolate you don't happen to like. You'll have to wait until your host offers you seconds if you want to try your luck again. If you're allergic to peanuts (or coconut or dairy products or whatever), you should stay away from mystery foods like assorted chocolates unless the box comes with a chart listing all the ingredients.

You're at a friend's house after school and smell lasagna cooking. You *adore* lasagna! You should . . .

A. smile and say "That lasagna smells delicious!" Then leave it at that, hoping your hint will be taken.

B. sit on the floor in front of the oven window, staring and drooling.

C. fib. Say your parents fell off the roof and are in body casts, and your grandma's staying with you, but she's a bad cook and makes burnt split-pea soup every night.

D. wander around the house loudly repeating "Mmm . . . I sure do *love* lasagna!" until you're invited to stay.

Answer: A. There's nothing wrong with dropping a little hint in a situation like this. But remember that a good hint is like a tap on the shoulder. A bad one is like a bonk on the head with a sledgehammer. If your hinting is too heavy-handed (see answers B, C, and D), you'll only annoy people. And that's no way to get invited to a lasagna dinner!

You're spending the night at a friend's house, and you start feeling very queasy and feverish. What should you do?

A. Nothing, because you don't want to insult your friend's parents' cooking.

B. Seize the chance to play a great prank. Barf in your friend's slippers and giggle like crazy when he or she slips them on.

C. Rummage quietly through the medicine cabinet for something that'll help you feel better, but don't say anything because you don't want to get sent home.

D. Tell your friend's parents how you feel, and ask them to call your parents.

Answer: D. If you're feeling seriously sick, it's serious business. This is no time for puking pranks or stupid secrets. You should let an adult know right away.

You've been doing science experiments at a friend's house, and it's time to go home. You . . .

A. help with the cleanup and say thanks as you leave.

B. dash out the door before someone hands you a mop.

C. hand your friend a dollar and say "Here's a tip. You clean up this mess."

D. tell your friend's little brother that if he doesn't clean up your mess, you'll turn him into a potato and eat him for dinner.

Answer: A. If you and your friend had been at your house instead, you would, of course, expect his or her help with the cleanup. And you'd think your friend was a real jerk if he or she bolted without helping or scared the daylights out of your little sibling. Act the same way you'd expect your friend to act, and you'll make sure he or she stays a friend.

I'll Get It— It's For Me!

Ring! . . . Ring!
"Hello?"
"Hello, may I speak to your mother, please?"
"Yeah, hold on . . . **MO-OMM!!**"

Hopefully the above scene isn't business as usual at your house. But if it rings true to you, why don't you try out this chapter and brush up on your telephone manners?

Use the telephone to . . .

A. call people and say "Is your refrigerator running? . . . Well, you'd better go chase it!" Then laugh and hang up.

B. make pretty music. Try to play "Twinkle, Twinkle, Little Star" by pressing numbers on the keypad.

C. make necessary calls only.

D. meet people from all over. Dial a "1" plus any ten numbers and see where your call ends up. Maybe you'll get Alaska!

Answer: C. It's true that telephones could be very entertaining if used creatively. So what's wrong with having a little phone fun? Well, for one thing, prank phone calls (answers A and D) are illegal. They're also mean. And did I mention expensive? Even if you're only playing a twinkly tune on the keypad, you could end up connecting with Timbuktu and ringing up a phone bill that'll take months of your allowance to pay!

A stranger calls and asks for your parents, who aren't home. You should . . .

A. say you've tied them up during a game of cops and robbers.

B. tell the caller that your parents are busy and offer to take a message.

C. call the police and beg them to send over a SWAT team to protect you.

D. say your parents aren't home and tell the caller exactly when they'll be back.

Answer: B. I'm sure you already know it's not safe to tell a strange caller your parents aren't home. But don't wig out, either. It's probably a perfectly normal call from a friend or coworker. Or it might be a sales or survey call. (Both can be annoying, but neither is dangerous.) Don't tell a silly fib that your parents may wind up having to explain later. Nor should you call the police, unless the stranger says something frightening. Just say your parents are busy. That way you'll be telling the truth and acting polite without giving out too much information.

You're trying to call your friend Anna, but the guy who answers the phone says there's no Anna living there. What do you do?

A. Slam down the phone. How embarrassing!

B. Ask "Are you sure? Absolutely sure? Absolutely, positively sure?"

C. Scream "What have you done with Anna?! I'm calling the police!"

D. say "I'm sorry. I must have dialed a wrong number."

Answer: D. It's easy to make a mistake when you're dialing a phone number. Sometimes your fingers slip, or you dial too fast, or you're playing a video game at the same time, or you remember the number incorrectly, or . . . Well, you get the idea. The point is: If the scenario above happens to you, it's 99.999999999% likely that you're the one who made the mistake, not the person who answered the phone. So apologize briefly and try dialing again—more carefully this time.

When you answer the phone and it's for your mom, . . .

A. yell "MO-OMM!" as loudly as you can.

B. bark "Who's this and whaddaya want?"

C. growl "This is Al's Alligator Ranch and Juice Bar. We ain't got no moms here."

D. say "Please hold on" and get your mom. If she's busy, say "I'm sorry; she can't come to the phone. May I take a message?"

Answer: D. Yelling into the phone (answer A) could destroy the eardrums of the poor person on the other end. Demanding the caller's name and purpose as in answer B will probably get you a lecture on treating people with respect. (If your mom likes to know who's calling, say "May I tell her who's calling?" instead.) As for answer C . . . If you can pull off that line without laughing, maybe you should go to Hollywood. (The walk would do you good!)

When you call a friend and somebody else answers the phone, . . .

A. say "Hi, this is ____. May I please speak to ____?"

B. get to know the person if you don't already. Ask about his or her health, favorite color, hobbies, and so on.

C. say "I don't wanna talk to *you*, you scum-sucking phone snatcher!"

D. say "I understand you're holding ____ hostage. Is the prisoner allowed phone calls?"

Answer: A. If you can't bring yourself to be polite simply because it's the nice thing to do, then do it because it's the only sure way to get your friend on the phone. Name-calling and sarcasm will probably just get you a dial tone. And yes, it is indeed possible to be too friendly sometimes. Instead of wasting people's time, get right to the point: Say hi, identify yourself, and ask for your friend by name.

Which of the following is okay to do?

A. Leave pizza grease, lip balm, or hair gel on the telephone receiver.

B. Talk on the phone while you're going to the bathroom.

C. Drop a cordless phone handset wherever you happen to finish your call.

D. Take the phone off the hook for two hours so no one can bother you.

Answer: None of the above. *If you leave grease or goop on the phone, be a pal and wipe it off with a damp cloth. (Not a dripping wet cloth—or you could get the shock of a lifetime!) Talking on the phone while going to the bathroom breaks the Golden Toilet Rule. (See page 60 and keep your peeing and pooping to yourself.) You should return a cordless phone handset to the base when you're done with it so no one has to hunt for it when the next call comes in. (Cordless phones have different kinds of batteries, so ask your parents if you should always put the handset on the base to recharge, or if you should recharge it only when the battery runs low.) Finally, leaving the phone off the hook for a long time isn't wise, because you never know when someone might need to get hold of you in an emergency.*

When you want to make a call and a sibling is on the phone, . . .

A. lurk nearby and look very impatient. Tap your foot, drum your fingers, point to your watch, and glare.

B. do something fun while you're waiting to help pass the time.

C. shoot rubber bands at your sibling until he or she gets mad and drops the phone.

D. pick up another extension and blow a whistle into the mouthpiece.

Answer: B. If you choose A, C, or D, expect the same treatment when it's your turn to use the phone.

You're on the phone, and your Call Waiting beeps in. You should . . .

A. answer it and shout "Go away!"

B. ignore it.

C. answer it while the first caller is talking. He or she won't even notice you've disappeared.

D. say "Please excuse me for a moment; that's our Call Waiting." Answer the second call and take a message as quickly as possible. (If it's an emergency, end the first call with an apology.)

Answer: D. Call Waiting makes it hard to always have good phone manners. When it beeps in on your phone, you have to answer it—that's why your parents installed it in the first place. But by doing so, you're telling the first caller that your time is more important than his or hers. You're also forcing the first caller to pick between two bad choices: hang there in limbo until you return or hang up on you. Troublesome though it is, Call Waiting isn't going to go away anytime soon. So we'll have to deal with it as best we can. If you have Call Waiting, answer it as quickly as possible and be sure to apologize when you ask someone to wait or need to end a call.

When you're taking a phone message, . . .

A. use pictures instead of words to make it fun and challenging to read.

B. don't worry about writing it down. You'll remember it just fine.

C. listen carefully, write clearly, and deliver the message or put it where it'll be found right away.

D. make a game of it. See if you can act so dumb that the caller yells at you. Collect one point for each swear word.

Answer: C. Let's pretend that your friend Josh calls to tell you tomorrow's science assignment while you're in the bathroom: You're supposed to collect five different kinds of leaves. Your sister takes a message for you. . . . Using plan A, she draws a hand and five things that look sort of like feathers. Using plan B, she tells you, "You're supposed to heckle five different hives of bees." Using plan D, the next morning she says, "What's Josh's problem, anyway? He called for you last night, but all he did was swear at me and hang up." . . . To avoid disasters like these, make sure that you (and everyone else in your family) write down messages clearly and correctly and deliver them right away.

You've been on the phone for over an hour. Your mom's standing there looking impatient. You should . . .

A. pretend you're talking about schoolwork so your mom will leave you alone.

B. sigh and say "I'm sorry to interrupt you, but my mom seems to want the phone. I guess what she wants is more important, so I'd better hang up." Then slam down the phone and storm out of the room.

C. say "Excuse me for a second" and ask your mom if she needs the phone. If so, explain it to your friend and hang up.

D. turn your back so you don't have to keep looking at you mom.

Answer: C. This may be hard to believe, but your mom really isn't out to ruin your life. And she does realize that your friendships are important. (That should be obvious if she's let you hog the phone for an hour already.) But like all good things, all great phone calls must come to an end. Let others have a turn to make their important phone calls now.

When you reach an answering machine, . . .

A. say "This is POW-POW-POWER radio, KPOW! You've won two tickets to this year's monster truck rally! We'll give you the whole seat, but you'll only need the edge!"

B. breathe heavily and hang up.

C. leave your name, phone number, the time you called, and a short message.

D. ramble on and on and on and on and on and on and on and on and on and . . .

Answer: C. "Hi, it's me. Don't forget to bring those thingamajigs tonight." Click. Have you ever gotten a message like this? You don't recognize the voice and you haven't a clue what the caller's talking about. In fact, you're not even sure the message is for you. If confusing answering-machine messages drive you nuts, then do your part to stamp them out. Always leave short, clear messages. Confusing and/or endless ones are irritating, and prank messages are just as illegal as prank calls.

The Star of the Audience

Why do all the eight-foot giants and armrest commandos come out only for events that cram hundreds of people together? Going to a movie or a live show is supposed to be fun but can sometimes be frustrating. Answer the questions in this chapter and find out how good you are at staying polite under pressure.

It's okay to whisper when . . .

A. you need to tell your parents something important at church, temple, or a show.

B. the man two rows up just picked his nose, and you want to be sure your sister catches him picking the other nostril.

C. your best friend is giving a speech in front of the class, and you want to tell him or her "Psst! Your zipper's open!"

D. you're telling a joke in class and you don't want your teacher to hear you.

Answer: A. If you're in a quiet place and you have something truly important to say (perhaps some little brat's about to let a frog loose in church), then whispering is all right. Whispering is also okay if you absolutely need to say something private right away. (Let's say you're having Thanksgiving dinner, and you need to tell your dad his tie's dunked in the gravy.) Just don't make a habit of it. Whispering jokes or other funny stuff while you're supposed to be listening to someone will hurt the speaker's feelings. As for alerting your friend to that wayward zipper . . . Don't do it in the middle of the speech! Wait until your friend sits down so he or she doesn't die of embarrassment.

There's a long line of people waiting to buy movie tickets. You . . .

A. walk right past everyone and into the theater, saying "It's okay; I work here."

B. point away from the theater and shout "Michael Jordan's signing autographs around the corner!"

C. shout a common name like Joe or Mary until someone at the front turns around. Then hop in line and pretend to know him or her until you're in the door.

D. wait by the theater's rear exit and sneak in when the early show lets out.

Answer: None of the above. Don't try any of these line-butting stunts unless you want to be chased by an angry mob, banned from every theater in town, and called Butthead for the rest of your life. You'll be much better off if you just wait in line like everyone else.

When you can't see past the people in front of you at a movie, you should . . .

A. toss Junior Mints at them until they get the mint—I mean hint.

B. yank their heads back and say "*Ahh . . . that's better!*"

C. keep saying "Did you see that? I didn't!" all through the movie.

D. move to another seat if possible.

Answer: D. It can be tough to be a kid at the movies. Sometimes it seems as if everyone in the theater is three times your size! Still, you should try not to lose your cool when a couple of giants sit down in front of you. Don't pester the giants—if you make them mad enough, they could squash you like a bug. Don't squirm or stand up or do anything to bother the people behind you, either—or they might use YOU for target practice! Just look for a better seat if you can. Or make a point of getting to the theater early so you can sit on the aisle.

If you get restless or bored at a movie, . . .

A. hug yourself and make kissing noises.

B. daydream or take a nap.

C. tap out a message in Morse code and keep doing it until someone answers.

D. toss popcorn in the air and try to catch it in your mouth. Each time you succeed, yell "He shoots . . . He scores!"

Answer: B. It's a bummer when you go to a movie and for some reason don't enjoy it. But it's not fair to let your restlessness or boredom ruin the show for everyone else. Just catch up on your sleep or plan your next birthday party until the movie's over.

It's okay to talk during a movie when . . .

A. you need to warn everyone of the really scary part coming up.

B. a rat has crawled onto your lap and is nibbling on your shirt.

C. the people around you are old and probably deaf.

D. two people in front of you are making out, and you want to give everyone a play-by-play account.

Answer: B. To avoid bothering other people, you should never talk during a movie—unless you've got a major emergency on your hands (or your lap!).

If you drop something on the floor during any sort of show, . . .

A. crawl around looking for it. You might find some other cool stuff, too.

B. shout "Anyone got a light?!"

C. forget about it unless it's something really important like your house key or wallet.

D. sob uncontrollably.

Answer: C. No matter how hard you try not to, you're going to annoy people by crawling around on the floor. So don't do it to look for a piece of candy, a lost tissue, or anything else that isn't important. (If you're tempted by the possibility of finding other cool stuff, remember that you're far more likely to find sticky puddles of spilled soda, used chewing gum, and year-old popcorn.) If the thing you've dropped is truly important, search as quickly as you can.

At a live show, . . .

A. try to distract the performers by making silly faces and noises.

B. if you miss something, ask the performers to repeat it. They love that!

C. sneak in your pet hamster and let it loose onstage to liven things up.

D. sing along with the music or join in with the dialogue, even if you have no idea what's going on.

Answer: None of the above. Live performers work hard to entertain you, so the least you can do is try not to make their job any harder than it already is. And always applaud at the end of a live show. Even if you didn't like it, the performers deserve to be thanked for their efforts.

You should leave your seat at a movie, show, or sports event . . .

A. by crawling under the other seats so you don't disturb anyone.

B. by announcing "Everybody up, please. Time for a pee break!"

C. in a way that will bother people as little as possible and only if it's absolutely necessary.

D. by tiptoeing carefully on the armrests between you and the aisle.

Answer: C. It's best to avoid leaving your seat at all, because you're going to bother a lot of people if you do. Buy treats and use the bathroom before the movie starts, and don't eat or drink so much during the movie that you need to use the bathroom again before it's over. If you absolutely, positively MUST get up, just walk out like a normal human being. Say "Excuse me" to each person you pass in your row and avoid stomping, brushing, bumping, or jabbing any of them.

When someone sitting in your row at a movie, show, or sports event needs to get past you, . . .

A. stand up or turn your legs to the side so the person can get by easily.

B. shoot out your leg at the last moment to trip the person.

C. scowl and say "Jeez, do you have a pint-sized bladder or something?"

D. hand the person two bucks and say "Hey, while you're up, I'll take a hot dog—no mustard."

Answer: A. Most people know they should try to stay seated at movies, shows, and sports events. So if someone in your row decides to get up, assume that he or she has a good reason. Don't embarrass, hurt, or otherwise slow the person down. What if he or she is sick? You might wind up getting barfed on!

139

You're the last person to leave a movie, show, or sports event, and you notice a purse under a seat. You should . . .

A. be grateful for the unexpected treasure. Take the money, but don't mess with the credit cards or prescription drugs, because only a dope touches that stuff.

B. take the purse to a theater employee.

C. hide items from the purse all over the theater. Put a note reading "Happy hunting!" inside the purse.

D. tell an usher "I think that purse is ticking."

Answer: B. If you've ever lost something important, you know how upsetting that can be. I'm sure you wouldn't dream of stealing money from a lost purse or playing a practical joke with it. Imagine the poor owner's reaction upon discovering nothing but a naughty note inside or being arrested for making a bomb threat. That's not funny; it's just plain mean!

What's Your Manners Quotient?

Congratulations on finishing the *What Do You Know about Manners?* quiz! I hope you've had fun along the way. I also hope you haven't been laughing too hard to keep track of your answers.

To find out your Manners Quotient (MQ), give yourself one point for each question you answered correctly. Subtract one point for any time you read a goofy wrong answer and decided to be a smart aleck and try it. Then compare your MQ with the chart on the next page.

So . . . how much do you really know about manners?

If your MQ is . . .	You should . . .
0 to 25	Check yourself into the zoo. With an MQ this low, you must be some sort of animal. You'll probably be happiest living in a place where all the residents are smelly and selfish, just like you.
26 to 50	Read this book again, v-e-r-y s-l-o-w-l-y. And this time, pay attention to the right answers, not the wrong ones! You're certainly not a lost cause, but you could use a refresher course in basic courtesy.
51 to 75	Keep it up. You're well on your way to being a manners star, and with some polishing, you'll really sparkle. With just a little more effort, you can help make the world a much brighter place.
76 to 100	Give yourself a standing ovation! People enjoy being around you because you're so good at re-membering the needs of others. It's not always easy, but you know it's worth the effort.

Index

Kids Pick the Funniest Poems

Edited by Bruce Lansky
Illustrated by Stephen Carpenter

Three hundred elementary-school kids will tell you that this book contains the funniest poems for kids—because they picked them! Not surprisingly, they chose many of the funniest poems ever written by favorites like Shel Silverstein, Jack Prelutsky, Bruce Lansky, Jeff Moss, and Judith Viorst. This book is guaranteed to please children ages 6–12.

Order #2410

No More Homework! No More Tests!

Edited by Bruce Lansky
Illustrated by Stephen Carpenter

This is the funniest collection of poems about school by the most popular children's poets, including Shel Silverstein, Jack Prelutsky, Bruce Lansky, David L. Harrison, Colin McNaughton, Kalli Dakos, and others who know how to find humor in any subject. (Ages 6–12)

Order #2414

Free Stuff for Kids 2000
by the Free Stuff Editors

This 4.7-million-copy bestseller is updated with new offers for the 21st century.

The 2000 edition of America's #1 kids' activity book contains more than 90% all-new offers. This latest edition will have fresh appeal to the hundreds of thousands of kids who bought last year's edition.

Free Stuff for Kids contains hundreds of free and up-to-a-dollar offers children can send away for through the mail.

Order #2190

**Look for Meadowbrook Press books where you buy books.
You may also order books by using the form printed below.**

Order Form

Qty.	Title	Author	Order No.	Unit Cost (U.S. $)	Total
	Bad Case of the Giggles	Lansky, B.	2411	$16.00	
	Craft Fun with Sondra	Clark, S.	3301	$5.95	
	Emperor's New Underwear	Anholt/Robins	2601	$3.95	
	Free Stuff for Kids	Free Stuff Editors	2190	$5.00	
	Just for Fun Party Games	Warner, P.	6065	$3.95	
	Kids Are Cookin'	Brown, K.	2440	$8.00	
	Kids' Party Cookbook	Warner, P.	2435	$12.00	
	Kids' Party Games & Activities	Warner, P.	6095	$12.00	
	Kids' Pick-A-Party Book	Warner, P.	6090	$9.00	
	Kids Pick the Funniest Poems	Lansky, B.	2410	$16.00	
	Kids' Outdoor Parties	Warner, P.	6045	$8.00	
	Miles of Smiles	Lansky, B.	2412	$16.00	
	No More Homework, Tests	Lansky, B.	2414	$8.00	
	Poetry Party	Lansky, B.	2430	$13.00	
	Silly Jack and the Beanstack	Anholt/Robins	2600	$3.95	
				Subtotal	
			Shipping and Handling (see below)		
			MN residents add 6.5% sales tax		
			Total		

YES! Please send me the books indicated above. Add $2.00 shipping and handling for the first book with a retail price up to $9.99 or $3.00 for the first book with a retail price over $9.99. Add $1.00 shipping and handling for each additional book. All orders must be pre-paid. Most orders are shipped within two days by U.S. Mail (7–9 delivery days). Rush shipping is available for an extra charge. Overseas postage will be billed.
Quantity discounts available upon request.

Send book(s) to:

Name _____ Address _____

City _____ State _____ Zip _____ Telephone (____)_____

Payment via:

❏ Check or money order payable to Meadowbrook Press

❏ Visa (for orders over $10.00 only)   ❏ MasterCard (for orders over $10.00 only)

Account # _____ Signature _____ Exp. Date _____

A FREE Meadowbrook Press catalog is available upon request.
You can also phone us for orders of $10.00 or more at 800-338-2232.

Mail to: Meadowbrook Press, 5451 Smetana Drive, Minnetonka, MN 55343
Phone 612-930-1100   Toll-Free 800-338-2232   Fax 612-930-1940

For more information (and fun) visit our website: www.meadowbrookpress.com